Karen's Logic Thinking Puzzles

Lateral Thinking Riddles and Brain Teasers for All Ages

Karen J. Bun

Table of Contents

Introduction
Chapter 1: What Is Lateral Thinking?
Chapter 2: Easy Lateral Thinking Puzzles and Brain Teasers

The Guarded Doors

The Murder

The Tricky Juice Glasses

Logical Fruits

Bankruptcy

Trapped in a Room

The Series

The Multiple Birth

Tea

Weight Loss

Thief

The Dark Room

Name Calling

Dangerous Trucking

The Writer

The Chicken Coop

The Crowd

The Solutions:

The Guarded Door

The Murder

The Tricky Juice Glasses

Logical Fruits

Bankruptcy

Trapped in a Room

The Series

The Multiple Birth

Tea

Weight Loss

Thief

The Dark Room

Name Calling

Dangerous Trucking

The Writer

The Chicken Coop

The Crowd

Chapter 3: Intermediate Lateral Thinking Puzzles and Brain Teasers

The Bee Holder

The 3 Sons

Pink

Imprisoned

Cowboy

The Dark Room

Parking Space

Sequence

The Bridge

The Rebus

Green-Eyed Logic

Cheryl's Birthday

Boxed Names

Love in Kleptopia

Cookies

The Monkey and the Coconuts

Flipping Coins

The Waiter

The Boxes

The Cannibals

The Three Princes

Solutions:

    The Bee Holder

    The 3 Sons

    Pink

    Cowboy

    The Dark Room

    Parking Space

Sequence

The Bridge

The Rebus

Green-Eyed Logic

Cheryl's Birthday

Boxed Names

Love in Kleptopia

Cookies

The Monkey and the Coconuts

Flipping Coins

The Waiter

The Boxes

The Cannibals

The Three Princes

Chapter 4: Advanced Lateral Thinking Puzzles and Brain Teasers

The Emperor

The Stark Raving Mad King

The Prison Warden

The Neighborhood

The Game Show

The Infinite Hotel

Pirates

Pirates II
The Greek Philosophers
The Bar Fly
Solutions:

    The Emperor

    The Stark Raving Mad King

    The Prison Warden

    The Neighborhood

    The Game Show

    The Infinite Hotel

    Pirates

    Pirates II

    The Greek Philosophers

    The Bar Fly

Conclusion

Bluesource And Friends

This book is brought to you by Bluesource And Friends, a happy book publishing company.

Our motto is **"Happiness Within Pages"**.

We promise to deliver amazing value to readers with our books.

We also appreciate honest book reviews from our readers.

Connect with us on our Facebook page www.facebook.com/bluesourceandfriends and stay tuned to our latest book promotions and free giveaways.

Don't forget to claim your FREE book
https://tinyurl.com/karenbrainteasers

Also check out our best seller book
https://tinyurl.com/lateralthinkingpuzzles

Introduction

Congratulations on downloading *Karen's Logic Thinking Puzzles: Lateral Thinking Riddles and Brain Teasers for All Ages*. We thank you for doing so!

The following chapters will discuss a wide variety of logic and lateral thinking puzzles and will also discuss some history behind the creation of these kinds of lateral thinking puzzles. These kinds of brain teasers are fun and do train your brain to use *linear logic*, which is a skill that can be applied to many life situations. Lateral thinking refers to finding a solution to a riddle through thinking out-of-the-box and looking at all different possibilities. Basically, we are using logic in a creative way. This is the opposite of *vertical logic*, which is defined such that only self-reinforcing information is given to support the line of reasoning—an example of this would be stating that if there is an equal force applied to both ends of a weak stick, then the stick will eventually break in the center.

This book is just one of the many sources you can find online, so I am truly grateful that you decided to refer to this one. Rest assured that you can gain all the useful knowledge that you need to be proficient on the subject matter. Good luck!

Chapter 1: What Is Lateral Thinking?

Lateral thinking is a way of "teasing" your brain into coming up with a solution to a problem or puzzle by a creative logical approach. It involves using the reasoning that is not immediately obvious. The origins of the term "lateral thinking" are believed to date back to the fable of King Solomon from the biblical times. In this fable, King Solomon is approached to solve the question of which woman is the maternal mother to an infant, which they both claim to be the mother of. King Solomon decides to test the women by suggesting that the easy solution is to cut the infant in half and then give one half to each claiming mother. The woman who was, in fact, the maternal mother immediately reacted with fear to this suggestion and then withdrew her claim to the infant, stating that she would rather see him be given to the other woman than watch him get harmed in any way. King Solomon then knew that the woman who did not wish to see the infant harmed was, in fact, the maternal mother. He came to this conclusion by using his test of lateral thinking or coming up with a creative solution.

Lateral thinking is often compared to critical thinking. These differ in the sense that critical thinking is generally defined as judging the value of a given statement and analyzing the statement for errors.

Lateral thinking is more involved with the 'movement value' of the information given—or rather analyzing how each fact and statement relates to one another—and in these relations forming new ideas or conclusions.

The physician/philosopher Edward De Bono is the individual credited with defining the term *lateral thinking*. He broke down the Lateral Thinking Model into four types of thinking:

1. Idea-generating thinking;
2. Focus tool-generating thinking to search for new ideas;
3. Harvest tool thinking to ensure value from generated ideas; and
4. Treatment tool thinking, which considers real-world constraints and grounds the creative process into reality.

Lateral thinking puzzles are a fun and interesting way to learn how to think somewhat differently from the traditional 1+1=2 or obvious logic patterns. Oftentimes, we find ourselves stuck in our thinking about a problem that we want to overcome. This is generally because we are thinking about the solution to the problem in only one direction. More effort focused into the same direction will not necessarily bring you to a different destination, or as the saying goes, "You cannot dig a hole in a different place by digging the same hole deeper." It may sound as though lateral thinking is very complicated, although it is based in a fairly simple model. It is simply attempting to see the same thing in several different ways.

Let's use the methods presented in the concept of lateral thinking to solve the following lateral thinking riddles and brain teasers!

Chapter 2: Easy Lateral Thinking Puzzles and Brain Teasers

Let's jump in with some easy lateral thinking puzzles and teasers.

The Guarded Doors

You approach two doors that are guarded by two men. One door leads to freedom, while the other will lead you into imprisonment. One guard can only speak the truth, while the other one will only tell lies. It is unknown whether they are the truth-teller or the liar. In order to get past the guards and find the door to freedom, you must determine which guard will point you to the "freedom" door. You can only ask one question to determine this. What should your question be?

The Murder

Four children each have five rocks with them. They are playing a game on the riverbank, where they have to throw the rocks into the river and hit the solid ground so that the rocks do not sink. The game plays out such that:

Kid 1 – Throws three rocks that hit the solid ground, but one did sink.

Kid 3 – Had a bad aim, and all rocks sunk.

Kid 4 – Had perfect aim, and all rocks hit solid ground.

Kid 2 – Was the winner, but he/she got struck in the head with a rock and died.

Who killed Kid 2?

The Tricky Juice Glasses

Arranged on a table across one another are six glasses of identical sizes—with half of them containing orange juice while the other half containing nothing. How can you move one glass and therefore arrange the glasses to be alternating between full glasses and empty ones?

Logical Fruits

There is a basket full of fruits, which is described as follows:

All but two are grapes.

All but two are apples.

All but two are oranges.

How many fruits and what kinds of fruits are in the basket?

Bankruptcy

A driver was pushing their car until suddenly, he arrived at a hotel and realized that he was bankrupt. How did the driver know this?

Trapped in a Room

You are trapped in a room with 3 exits. Behind the first door, there is a bloodthirsty lion. Behind the second one exists a huge magnifier that reflects the sun rays and burns anything that walks past it. Behind the third door, there is a pit of poisonous snakes. Which door can you use to escape the room?

The Series

Which character should fill the blank?

W L C N I T __

The Multiple Birth

A woman gives birth to two babies who are delivered exactly on the same hour, day, and year—however, as it turns out, the two of them aren't twins. Why?

Tea

A man was drinking tea when suddenly, he was momentarily blinded. How did this happen?

Weight Loss

A man enters a room. He pushes one button. He instantly is 20 lb. lighter. How did this happen?

Thief

A woman walks through a department store while pushing a cart. She fills up the cart with many items until the cart is overflowing. She leaves the store without paying for anything, and no one attempts to stop her even though many employees see her. How did she do this?

The Dark Room

A man is sitting alone in a dark room quietly enjoying himself. Suddenly, he begins to choke and cannot breathe. Soon after, his ability to breathe returns to normal, and he goes back to enjoying himself. What happened?

Name Calling

A woman hears her name called and then is taken away by two men. Later on, she dies in the care of many. Why did this happen?

Dangerous Trucking

A trucking company uses the same employees and runs the same routes every day. There is not ever an issue with traffic accidents or later deliveries. They decide to do deliveries on Christmas Day to generate more business. When Christmas Day came, the drivers were sent out on their usual route. Later on that day, the dispatchers received a call that one of the drivers had struck a bridge and severely damaged the truck. How could this have happened if the trucks were using the same routes they always had without issues?

The Writer

Every two weeks, a man sits down and writes two words on each piece of 60 pages of paper. Why does he do this?

The Chicken Coop

A farmer has a chicken coop with twelve egg-producing hens. One night, a huge storm comes and kills all but eight of the chickens. How many chickens does the farmer have in the morning?

The Crowd

David enters a restaurant where many people are eating and socializing. When the diners see him, they drop their forks and run away. Why did they do this?

The Solutions:

The Guarded Door

"What door would the other guard say leads to freedom?" And whatever answer you get, do the opposite. If you happen to ask the truth teller, he will accurately tell you the response of the lying guard (which will be the opposite of the truth so just do the opposite). If you happen to ask the liar, he will lie about the truthful statement that the other guard would give (therefore also resulting in telling you the opposite of the truth so just do the opposite).

The Murder

The murderer is Kid 1, as he has one rock left over after the rock-pitching game.

The Tricky Juice Glasses

Pick up the second juice glass, and then pour all the juice from it into the fifth glass. Then, put the second glass back to its original position.

Logical Fruits

There are three fruits—one apple, one grape, and one orange.

Bankruptcy

The man was playing Monopoly.

Trapped in a Room

Using the second door, exit the room in the evening. There is no sun at night, so the magnifying glass will be harmless.

The Series

The last letter is S. The letters series are the first letters taken from the instruction "What Letter Comes Next in This Series?"

The Multiple Birth

The two babies were two of triplets.

Tea

The man left a spoon in the teacup. When he drank from the mug, the handle of the spoon poked him in the eye, momentarily blinding him.

Weight Loss

The man entered an elevator and pushed the 'UP' button. When the elevator moved upwards, he felt lighter as the air pressure changed.

Thief

The woman was a janitor working in the department store. She was filling up a cart with garbage bags. When the cart was full, she left the store to throw the garbage into the trash compactor.

The Dark Room

The man was sitting in a movie theatre. He was having a drink with ice cubes in it. One of the ice cubes got stuck in his throat, momentarily choking him. The ice cube would have then melted, allowing him to breathe normally again.

Name Calling

The woman was in a courtroom and was convicted of a crime. She was sentenced to the death penalty. The man who called her name was the judge, and the men who led her off were the prison guards. She later died in prison surrounded by family and the prison staff.

Dangerous Trucking

On Christmas Day, many businesses are closed. Because of this, the truck driver was not able to complete his usual amount of deliveries and still had goods on his truck when he made the return trip to the home office. As such, the truck bed was at a higher elevation than it would have been if he had been returning with an empty truck as usual. Because of the higher truck bed, the driver struck a bridge on his usual route back, which he ordinarily would have been able to pass underneath with an empty truck bed.

The Writer

The man is the owner of a company with 60 employees. Every two weeks, he writes his first and last name on their paychecks.

The Chicken Coop

The farmer still has twelve chickens. Eight are dead, and four are alive. The dead chickens are still in the chicken coop.

The Crowd

David is not a person—he is a boa constrictor who escaped from the zoo and wandered into a restaurant.

Chapter 3: Intermediate Lateral Thinking Puzzles and Brain Teasers

Let's dig deeper with some more intricate lateral thinking puzzles and brain teasers.

The Bee Holder

If I am holding a bee in my hand, what must be in my eye?

The 3 Sons

David's father has three sons. Two are named Stan and Steve. What is the other son's name?

Pink

In one pink single-level dwelling—with walls, floors, furniture, and drapes all colored pink—there lives a woman. What color are the stairs?

Imprisoned

You are imprisoned and given a deal to escape. If you can choose which of the three escape doors will not lead to your death, you are then freed with a full pardon. Your choices are as follows:

1. A door with a lion behind it that has not been fed in months
2. A door which leads into an inferno
3. A door which leads to a trainer sniper shooter

Which door do you pick?

Cowboy

A cowboy leaves town on Friday and takes up residence somewhere else for three days. He then returns to town on Friday. How is this possible?

The Dark Room

You're trapped inside some room without any lighting and only with one match, one candle, a gas lamp, and a gas stove. Which item should you light first?

Parking Space

In the diagram below, what is the number of the parking spot that the car is parked in?

Sequence

In the following sequence, what is the next number?

1, 11, 21, 1211, 111221, 312211, _____?

The Bridge

Four people must cross a narrow bridge to get across a river. The bridge can only hold two people at a time, or it will break. As it is nighttime, they must use a torch to get across the bridge safely. The torch will stay lit only for 15 minutes. When two people cross the bridge together, they must move at the slower person's pace. The pace of all four people is as follows:

Person A – cross the bridge in one minute

Person B – cross the bridge in two minutes

Person C – cross the bridge in five minutes

Person D – cross the bridge in eight minutes

How can they all get across the bridge in less than 15 minutes as to not lose the torchlight?

The Rebus

The following 'Rebus' or pictogram represents the saying 'See Eye-to-Eye'

'Ci ii"

What do the following Rebus puzzles mean?

1. important=important

2. U R YY 4 me

3. MOUNT MOUNT MOUNT MOUNT MOUNT MOUNT MOUNT MOUNT MOUNT MOUNT

4. A4id

5. NIPs

6. THAT'S

    RATED

7. D   B#1
   N   B#2
   A   B#3
   T   B#4
   S   B#5

8. ~~O~~ GOOD
        TV

9. Give Get
   Give Get
   Give Get
   Give Get

10. STANDS
    0_23456789

Green-Eyed Logic

A cruel dictator runs an island. He has imprisoned 100 people on this island. All of these prisoners are perfect logicians. There are rules on this island that all prisoners follow for fear of being either tossed into one of the many volcanoes or chucked out to drown in the shark-infested waters that surround the island. There is only one potential method of escape from this island. This method is to simply ask one of the guards to be released. The caveat is that the guard will only release the prisoner if the prisoner has green eyes. If not, the prisoner will be thrown into a volcano. What the prisoners do not know is that all 100 of them have green eyes. They do not know this because of a few facts:

1. They have all been on the island since birth.
2. They cannot communicate with one another through either written or verbal communication, though they do all see each other in the headcount, which is done every morning.
3. There are no reflective surfaces on the island, and the prisoners will not go near the water for fear of the sharks.
4. All liquids are served only in opaque containers.
5. They all also know that no prisoner would ever attempt to leave without complete certainty of success.

Life moves along on the dictator's island for many years. Then, many human rights groups become interested in the island and begin to protest for the dictator to be overthrown and the prisoners to be set free. The dictator reluctantly agrees to let one human rights representative onto the island to show that the prisoners are not being treated inhumanely. He imposes a few rules onto the representative under the threat of being thrown into the volcano. The rules are as follows:

1. The representative may only speak one sentence to the prisoners.
2. The representative may not tell the prisoners any new information.

The representative thinks all night and then comes up with a perfect statement that will help the prisoners in freeing them all.

After the representative speaks to the prisoners, she is allowed to leave the island safely, as what she said was deemed permissible by the dictator. Then, ninety-nine nights go by. On the one-hundredth morning, all of the prisoners are free.

What did the representative say to the prisoners without invoking the dictator's wrath and which aided in their freedom?

Cheryl's Birthday

Cheryl has become friends with Steve and Rick. They both ask her the date of her birth. She then provides ten probable ones.

15th, 16th, or 19th of May
17th or 18th of June
14th or 16th of July
14th, 15th, or 17th of August

Afterward, she gives Steve the day, then fills in Rick with the month. The next day, Steve and Rick have this conversation:

Steve: I don't know for sure what is the exact date of Cheryl's birthday.

Rick: Same here.

Steve: Initially, it was unknown to me as well—however, I do now.

Rick: If that's the case, I know the date of her birth now as well.

What's the date of her birth?

Boxed Names

There are 100 inmates in a prison. Each of the inmates' names is written on a piece of paper and placed into a wooden box. The paper is only visible by opening the box completely. One by one, the inmates are led into the room containing the boxes. Each inmate is permitted to look inside 50 boxes, though they must not be moved or rearranged in any way, as the room must be left exactly the way it was found. Each inmate is not permitted to have any communication about the room with any other inmate. Before this process commences, the inmates are allowed a small amount of time to discuss their strategy of looking through the boxes as they are given a challenge. If each inmate can find his own name in the boxes, then all will be set free. If they cannot each find their own names, they will all be executed.

What is the best possible solution that would give them at least a 30% chance of succeeding?

Love in Kleptopia

Dave and Laura have fallen in love via the internet. Dave wishes to send Laura a ring through the mail. They both live in the country of Kleptopia where anything sent through the mail will be certainly stolen. The only way to protect anything against theft is if it is in a padlocked box. Both Dave and Laura have many padlocks, but neither one of them has a key to the padlock the other owns. How can Dave get the ring safely to Laura?

Cookies

In a family of four, the sons and daughters were bought cookies by their mom and dad, who were then keeping the money for them to purchase some markdown-priced cookies that are a few days past their "Best Before" dates. At full price, they also purchased 2 pieces that are not expired.

When they get home with the cookies, the kids both grab two. They do not check which is which, so they could have either the expired or the fresh cookies. Is there a better chance that they ended up with the fresh cookies, or is there an equal chance that they could have gotten either the fresh or the expired cookies?

The Monkey and the Coconuts

On an inhabited island, 10 persons are stranded in which, to their luck, they stumble upon a monkey as well as many coconuts. They filled their coconut storage on their first day. This is hard work, so after finishing the task, they then go in slumber and gave each of themselves an equal portion (1/10) of their total food supplies the day after. Early in the morning, one of the castaways wakes before the others. He is hungry and decides to take a coconut for himself before the distribution happens. He distributes the coconuts into the ten equal piles then realizes that one pile is short. He then sees a nearby monkey holding a coconut. If he is to take the monkey's coconut, he will have enough coconuts to make ten equal piles. He attempts to take the coconut from the monkey, but the monkey bonks him over the head with the coconut—thus killing him instantly. None of the other castaways is aware that this has happened. A bit later on, another castaway wakens and finds the killed castaway lying dead near the coconut piles. He sees this as an opportunity to get more coconuts for him since one of the castaways is now dead. He then divides the coconuts into nine equal piles but also comes up with one short. The monkey is nearby once again, still holding the one coconut that he used to kill the first castaway. The second castaway attempts to take this coconut from the monkey, and the monkey once again kills the castaway by bonking him on the head with a coconut. This pattern continues as each castaway awakens and then attempts to take the one coconut away from the monkey. There is now only the tenth castaway left alive who has the entire pile of the coconuts alone. How many coconuts are there at the minimum, excluding the one that the ape used as a murder weapon?

Flipping Coins

Lying above the table are 20 coins, which are identically distributed in such a way that 10 coins would be heads and the remaining ones would be tails. Now, the thing is that your eyes and hands are covered, so in turn, you cannot precisely describe the markings on the coins using your significantly reduced sense of touch. The goal is to separate them into 2 different classifications, with both of them having the same instances of tails and heads compared to one another. You are only allowed as far as flipping them as well as moving them to another group. What should you do in order to achieve the goal required?

The Waiter

Inside some random café, 3 guys buy a dish worth 15 dollars, from which every one of them pitches in 5 dollars. After receiving the payment from the server, the cook recognizes the customers as his buddies, prompting him to give back 5 dollars to them. Being untrustworthy and challenged in terms of Math, the server decided to just return $1 to every guy then take the remaining 2 dollars straight to his pocket. Hence, the 3 customers paid 4 dollars individually, making their combined payment 12 dollars. Including the 2 dollars that the server took, the total is 14 dollars. If the customers originally paid 15 dollars, what happened to the missing $1?

The Boxes

3 boxes are labeled as APPLES, ORANGES, and APPLES AND ORANGES, respectively. However, it is known to you how these labels are wrong, so you then let a friend get something in your chosen box. By picking just this, what can you possibly do to make the box's labels right?

The Cannibals

Through utilizing a boat that's only fit for 2 passengers, 3 cannibals & 3 anthropologists are expected to find a way to row across some random river. However, as a condition from the 3 cannibals, there should be no such instance when the anthropologists are outnumbered by the cannibals, lest they would get consumed as food.

How can they satisfy this condition and reach their goal at the same time?

The Three Princes

There once was a king who wanted his princess daughter to marry the most intelligent prince in the land. He gathered three princes who each declared themselves the most intelligent. The king gave them all a test to see the level of their intelligence and logic. He sat the three princes in a room—all facing one another while being blindfolded after being shown three black and two white hats. On the princes' heads, one headwear is placed, while the other ones unused are kept someplace else. Afterward, the monarch informed the three princes that he will remove their blindfolds and ask them to deduce the color of the hat that they are wearing without removing the hat or looking at their reflection in any way. The prince that concludes correctly the color of hat he is wearing will be awarded the princess's hand in marriage.

You are one of the princes. When the blindfolds are removed, you see two white hats on the other two princes in the room. Some time goes by without anyone saying anything. You begin to infer that two princes failed to figure out their assigned colors or can possibly be unable to venture a deduction. Can you tell what color is your hat?

Keep in mind that you know that both of your opponent princes are very intelligent, and just like you do, they very much aspire to marry the princess.

Solutions:

The Bee Holder

This is a play on words of the saying, "Beauty is in the eye of the beholder." If the bee is in your hand, you are the Beholder. Therefore, what is in your eye is *Beauty*.

The 3 Sons

The third son's name is David, as David's father has the three sons.

Pink

As Pink lives in a one-story house, there would not be any stairs.

Cowboy

The horse the cowboy is riding on is named Friday. Thus, he is able to leave on Friday and return on Friday even with just three days elapsing between.

The Dark Room

The first item you should light is the match.

Parking Space

The car is parked in space 87. The numbers are flipped upside-down from the viewer's perspective. They go in sequence: 86, 87, 88, 89 and 90.

Sequence

The next number is 13112221. The sequence is determined by each term in the sequence consisting of groups of two numbers based on the term previous to it. The first digit specifies the quantity, and the second digit specifies which digit.

For example, the first digit is 1, which has a 1 in it. Therefore, the next term is one-one, which is 11. This term has two ones in it, which is 21. This term has one-two and one-one, which is 1211. Keep these going, and you get the sequence.

The Bridge

The group can cross the bridge as determined in the two charts below in two ways:

Timing	Starting Side	Person/People crossing	Ending Side
0 minutes	A B C D		
2 minutes	C D	A and B cross (2 min)	A B
3 minutes	A C D	A returns (1 min)	B
11 minutes	A	C and D cross (8 min)	B C D
13 minutes	A B	B returns (2 min)	C D
15 minutes		A and B cross (2 min)	A B C D

Timing	Starting Side	Person / People crossing	Ending Side
0 minutes	A B C D		
2 minutes	C D	A and B cross (2 min)	A B
4 minutes	B C D	B returns (2 min)	A
12 minutes	B	C and D cross (8 min)	A C D
13 minutes	A B	A returns (1 min)	C D
15 minutes		A and B cross (2 min)	A B C D

The Rebus

1. Equally important
2. You are too wise for me
3. Mountain (mount times ten)
4. Foreign Aid
5. Reverse Spin
6. That's Overrated

7. Stand Up and Be Counted
8. Nothing Good on TV
9. Forgive and Forget
10. No One Understands

Green-Eyed Logic

The statement that the representative can make to help the prisoners without invoking the dictator's wrath is **"At least one of you has green eyes."**

Once the representative made the statement, the prisoners knew that at least one of them had the chance to be released with an absolute chance of success. They simply had to wait it out to see who would act first. The number of prisoners is arbitrary to the logical solution. Let us use an example as if there were only two prisoners, Greg and Paul. Greg and Paul both know that the other has green eyes, and the statement made by the representative confirms this. Therefore, they wait one day. If they are both still there after the one day passes, they can be sure that they both have green eyes and therefore have an absolute successful chance of being released from the island. If, for instance, Grey had blue eyes, Paul could see this and would know right away that he was the one with green eyes. He would have left and asked for freedom immediately. However, because they are both still there after one day had passed, they both now know that they both have green eyes, and therefore, both can be freed. Multiply this logic by the one hundred prisoners, and this explains why on the ninety-ninth night, all the island prisoners were free after having asked for their freedom.

Cheryl's Birthday

Cheryl's Birthday is July 16th. The statements made by the two boys deduce this. Rick only knows the month of Cheryl's birthday. He does not know the date. What he says first is a redundant statement. The only way that Steve could know the date of Cheryl's birthday is if she gave 18 or 19. These are solely the ones that make an appearance one time (19th of May as well as 18th of June). To be able to tell that it is unknown to Steve, Cheryl probably gave Rick July or August, as doing so would erase the possibility that Steve was told 18 or 19. Then comes the second line of the conversation when Steve says that he at first did not know, though now he does. Steve has reasoned that Rick knows either July or August. Should Rick actually know its actual date, he would've been given either 15, 16, or 17 since if he had been told 14 (the only other number choice), he would not know the month of Cheryl's birthday. The 15, 16, and 17 options all refer to one specific month, though the 14 could be either of the months. Then, when Rick states that he also now knows the date of Cheryl's birthday, he has confirmed that he has been told July. If he had been told August, he would not have been able to make the deduction of the number date being 16. Therefore, the date of birth is July 16th.

Boxed Names

In order to get at least a 30% chance of success, the inmates must make the concession that all of the boxes are labeled randomly by their own names. Each inmate then inspects the box labeled with his name and opens it. He then looks into the box which is labeled as according to the name, he just found until he finds his own name or until he has opened 50 boxes. If each inmate does this, they have created at least a 30% chance that they will be freed.

Love in Kleptopia

In order for Dave to safely get the ring to Laura, he must first send her the package with one of his padlocks on it. Then, once Laura has received the package, she does not attempt to open it—rather, she attaches one of her own padlocks to the package. She then sends the package with two padlocks on it back to Dave. Once Dave receives the package back, he removes his own padlock to which he has the key, and then he sends it back to Laura with only her padlock on it. Once Laura has received the package now with only her padlock on it, she can open it safely and receive the ring that Dave intended for her.

Cookies

The kids will end up with four possible results:
1. Kid 1 and 2 will each have 2 fresh cookies
2. Kid 1 and 2 will have 2 expired cookies
3. Kid 1 had 1 fresh cookie and 1 expired cookie.
4. Kid 2 had 1 fresh cookie and 1 expired cookie.

Therefore, there are equal chances of the kids getting fresh or expired cookies.

The Monkey and the Coconuts

The smallest number of coconuts that are left (not counting the monkey's murder weapon coconut) is 2519. This is determined by the Lowest Common Multiple (LCM) of 10,9,8,7,5,4,3,2,1 -1. LCM is the lowest numeral that's dividable using the given digits, and taking off 1 does yield the total of coconuts because we are not considering the one that the surviving monkey possesses.

Flipping Coins

Move the coins around into two piles with 10 each. Then, turn over everything from the first set, then put aside the second one. Set 1 will yield an equal count of tails and heads if compared to Set 2.

The Waiter

The money that the customers gave must be reflected on the receipt. It's senseless that what they gave (12 dollars) was added to the money in the server's pocket (2 dollars).

To make it clear, the customers paid 12 dollars. On the other hand, the establishment received 10 dollars as official payment, while the waiter has the 2-dollar remainder. This makes both the "paid" and "received" amounts equal to each other.

The Boxes

You must instruct your friend to choose one coming from the box labeled APPLES & ORANGES. It should have either only oranges or only apples. In the case that your buddy gets an orange, tag its box as ORANGES. Then, alter the ORANGES box to APPLES, and alter the APPLES box to APPLES & ORANGES.

The Cannibals

The primary thing to do is to let the 2 cannibals pass through and then instruct one of them to come back with the boat. Afterward, let 2 anthropologists pass through, and then one anthropologist follows a cannibal back—so now, there is one cannibal and one anthropologist on the far side of the river. The last two anthropologists go over to the far side, thus letting all anthropologists go across the other side, along with the boat and one cannibal. In the remaining two trips, the cannibal on the far side takes the boat and ferries the other two cannibals across the river.

The Three Princes

The hat that you, the prince, are wearing is white.

This is because your father wouldn't have selected 2 white hats as well as a black one, as it'd create a disadvantage to the prince wearing the black hat, as the 2 remaining ones are going to see a piece of each color. The king wants all three princes to have an equal chance of winning the wager. If you were the prince with black, then one of the others could easily deduce that he himself has a white one. Therefore, should a prince perceive that there is only a black hat, he can then easily deduce that he's the prince with the white one. Remember that their king started out by showing the three white hats and the two black hats.

Thus, it would only be just to let them all wear the three white headwear. This becomes apparent, as no one ventures an answer for some time. If the answer was obvious as described above, then one of the princes would most likely have answered immediately. However, because no one speaks right away, the safe assumption is that all three princes are wearing white hats.

Chapter 4: Advanced Lateral Thinking Puzzles and Brain Teasers

Now that we have had some fun with easy and intermediate lateral thinking puzzles, let us dive deeper with more advanced lateral thinking puzzles.

The Emperor

An emperor is scheduled to celebrate. This celebration is the biggest one held throughout history. There are 1000 bottles of wine that are planned to be opened. However, the emperor learns about one of these being toxic.

It will exhibit zero signs, though it will kill whoever consumes it. The person who intakes it will definitely die from 10–20 hours upon consumption.

The emperor has thousands of slaves as well as 1 day left to discover which of his bottles is toxic.

Meanwhile, they are scheduled to execute inmates, and no one else can be killed, lest the emperor's event will be compromised.

How many inmates have to check (through drinking) the wine for them to be certain that the poisoned bottle would be found within the given time limit?

The Stark Raving Mad King

There exists some random kingdom in which the king is stark raving mad. He gathers up the 100 wisest men and tells them that a blue or red hat was to be put on top of their heads. He will then line them up in no particular order. Once they are arranged, the men are forbidden to talk or make any communication through any means, and they are also not given the freedom to view other people from their backs or their own heads.

Meanwhile, they are allowed to view those in front of them, while they can only hear the answers of the ones at the back.

The inquiry will begin at the back, and the only acceptable answers are either "blue" or "red." Death will instantly fall upon anyone who would give a wrong response, while salvation will come if otherwise (although still required to keep their mouth shut). Another participant will then be asked. While their king starts raving mad, he does not make it clear why he is doing this, though he does clarify that breaking the rules would result to all of them getting called. Before they start, he lets the participants talk about their strategy, while he eavesdrops on them to determine whether they plan something fishy or not. In spreading the answer between the wise men, they can somehow cough or signal without breaking the rules and causing the death of them all.

How many of them (at most) are possibly able to survive?

The Prison Warden

Twenty-three new prisoners arrive on a prison. The warden welcomes them upon arrival, informing them that it is this very day alone that they are allowed to talk among themselves and form a way to somehow get out before they are locked into isolation the day after.

He then informs them:

"In here, there exists one switch room that has 2 switches with labels A and B, which can either be set up as 'up' or 'down.' The current locations of these items will be unknown to you, nor are they conveniently linked to anything. Starting tomorrow, at which every instance I feel like it, I'm going to randomly choose someone from you all then allow him to visit the switch room. In there, he will be given the freedom of choosing an option then required to put it in the opposite configuration ('up' or 'down') before being escorted out. The switches are to remain at their current state until the next participant is given their chance, in which I can arbitrarily choose anyone, including the ones already done. And don't worry—this isn't a ploy to kill you one at a time because I can do so right here and right now if it was truly my intention. Within the given period, every prisoner is supposed to enter the room as frequently as everyone else. At the exact moment you have already achieved this condition, you can inform me about this accomplishment, and your freedom shall be granted if this is proven to be factual—otherwise, death shall fall upon everyone without mercy. The rules are absolute and will be strictly enforced through every last strand of my power, and there shall be no instance when you can break them and come alive afterward."

What strategy can the prisoners come up with to all be set free?

The Neighborhood

In a neighborhood, there are five houses—each one a different color from the other. Every single one of them houses a person with another nationality, owns a different pet, prefers a different beverage, and smokes a different type of cigar. Using the following facts about the houses and their occupants, determine which house owner has a fish for a pet:

1. No owners have the same pet, drink the same beverage, or smoke the same type of cigar.
2. Situated inside the red house is the Brit.
3. The Swede has a dog as a pet.
4. Tea is favored by the Dane resident.
5. Situated on the left of White house is the Green house.
6. Coffee is preferred by the one who lives in the Green house.
7. A Paul Mall-smoking house owner has birds as pets.
8. A Dunhill-smoking owner lives in the Yellow house.
9. The center house's owner drinks milk.
10. The first house is occupied by the Norwegian resident.
11. The Blends-smoking person resides alongside the resident with a cat as a pet.
12. The house owner with horses resides beside the Dunhill-smoking homeowner.
13. The Blue Master-smoking resident prefers beer.
14. The German homeowner smokes Prince.
15. The Norwegian lives next to the blue house.
16. The resident who smokes Blends has a neighbor who drinks water.

Which of the house owners has a fish for a pet?

The Game Show

You are a contestant on a game show. You have made it into the final round, where you can win the grand prize of a car. You simply have to choose between three doors—one of which has a car behind it. In case you pick the one in front of a car, you're declared as the winner. The other two doors have a goat behind them. You decide to choose Door 2. The game show host opens Door 1 and reveals a goat behind it. The host then asks you if you want to stay with your choice of Door 2 to win the car or if you want to switch your choice and actually choose Door 3.

Will switching your choice of which door has the car behind it increase or decrease your chances of winning?

The Infinite Hotel

There is a hotel with an infinite amount of rooms that can safely be rented to an infinite amount of guests. The receptionist does not keep a schedule or tracking system to determine which guest is in each room, as there is always a room available due to the hotel's infinite nature. One night, when the hotel is very busy, a lone guest comes into the lobby. He asks if the hotel can rent him a room for the night. The receptionist knows that there is at least one room available, though as he does not keep a schedule or tracking system, he cannot immediately determine which room he can rent to the guest. He can, however, determine which room is available by making one simple announcement to all the guests currently in the hotel, and then rent the vacant room to the lone guest. What can this announcement be?

Pirates

There are 5 overly selfish and cunning pirates who aim to distribute their stolen one hundred gold coins amongst themselves, as proposed by their much more selfish captain. Everyone keys in their respective vote—and a majority of "aye" answers would render the proposal officially approved. Generally, whatever the captain proposes is accepted, as no pirate would have much of a chance to go up against the captain unless he had strong backing. In the case that the captain does not achieve a majority status (including himself), a mutiny is bound to arise, making all his cohorts fight him and choose a new leader for themselves.

Determine the highest possible number of coins that the leader is allowed to have that wouldn't trigger a mutiny and therefore risk his life.

Pirates II

The five previously mentioned pirates are joined by a sixth, and together, they enjoy a satisfying plundering of a rival ship that only has a few gold coins on it.

After they argue about the futility of killing an entire ship's crew for just one gold coin, they now must decide on a way to divide it.

Their three most important priorities are as follows:

1. Survival
2. Obtaining anything of monetary value
3. Death of rival pirates

Therefore, should a situation arise where the sum of money would essentially be the same, the pirates are keener to select the choice entailing the death of other pirates.

What can the pirate captain do to ensure that he lives through the decision of how to divide the last gold coin?

The Greek Philosophers

On a sunny morning, 3 philosophers from Greece were resting beneath a large tree. They had a long discussion about the meaning of life and their existence. They opened a bottle of wine and shared it amongst the three of them, and then each drifted off to sleep. A short while later, three owls came to rest among the philosophers and dropped a special present onto their heads. The owls then hooted and flew away. The noise awoke the three philosophers. The three of them shared looks with one another and burst to laughter. Afterward, a philosopher suddenly halted. What is the reason?

The Bar Fly

Upon entering a bar and finding his seat, a man was approached by the bartender and was asked what he would like. The man says, "A glass of water, please." The bartender pours him a glass of water, and the man takes a drink. He then pushes it away and says, "That's not enough." The bartender then held the man at gunpoint, to which the man responded, "Perfect, thank you!" He then leaves the bar.

Why would the bartender do this?

Solutions:

The Emperor

The smallest amount of inmates needed to drink from the wine to find the poisoned bottle is 10. This would be done as follows:

Label all bottles of wine with binary numbers, and then represent every single one of the inmates with the corresponding binary labels. Each inmate is required to go through the one specifically assigned to them.

Illustrated below is the mechanism in determining which of the following is the one that's toxic.

	1	2	3	4	5	6	7	8
Inmate A		x		x		x		x
Inmate B			x	x			x	x

Inmate C						x	x	x

The death of everyone would entail that the poison is in bottle 8. The survival of everyone would imply that bottle 1 is the one that's toxic. In the case that Inmate A and Inmate B both die, it can be inferred that the one that is toxic is bottle 4.

Considering that there are 10 inmates, it would result in 1024 different possible configurations—hence, they could try as much as 1024 bottles.

Everyone is bound to take a taste from around 500 bottles, and every trial must last for 15 seconds at most. This will ensure that if each inmate is only consuming about one millimeter of each bottle, then by the time the experiment is done, each inmate will have consumed around a bottle. Therefore, the chance of every inmate to survive is 50%.

The Stark Raving Mad King

There can be 99 wise men saved.

There could be about 50% of the men saved by everyone simply guessing randomly.

There could be about 50% of the men also saved if every even-numbered man in line heeds the request of saying the hat color that they face. In this manner, their respective hat colors will be known to the men, and they will survive. In the case that the one at the back does have an identical hat color (and there is a 50% chance of that happening), then both people will survive.

So how can 99 be saved?

They will need to follow this pattern:

Man 1 takes into account every red-colored hat he passes by (Q), then he responds "blue" in the case that the total red-colored hats that he encountered are odd. Meanwhile, he responds "red" in the case that the total number of red-colored hats that he encountered is even. Everyone else that follows takes into account the number of red-colored hats saved from the back (X) as well as those in front (Y).

In the case that Q was even, and if X and Y are either both even or are both odd, then the wise man would answer "blue." Otherwise, the wise man would answer "red."

If Q was odd and if X and Y are either both even or are both odd, then the wise man would answer "red." Otherwise, the wise man would answer "blue."

There can be any number of red-colored hats, as the chart below illustrates:

Wise Man	Hat He Wears	# of Red Hats He Sees	Red Hats Saved For Sure	He Answers
1	red	6	0	red
2	blue	6	0	blue
3	red	5	1	red
4	blue	5	1	blue
5	blue	5	1	blue

6	red	4	1	red
7	red	3	2	red
8	red	2	3	red
9	red	1	4	red
10	red	0	5	red

The Prison Warden

The prisoners will follow this strategy to be set free:

A leader is chosen among them, who then lives by these guidelines:

1. The completion of the task can only be broadcasted by their designated leader.
2. Everyone (besides their chosen leader) are supposed to flip up the first switch on their first try and again during the second one.
3. In the case that the first switch is already up or that they have already flipped it up twice, they will flip the second switch.

4. The first switch can only be flipped down by their designated leader—and in the case that the first switch is already down, then the second switch is to be flipped by the leader.
5. The number of times that he has flipped down the first switch should be taken into account by their designated leader.
6. Upon completing 44 switch-downs, their designated leader is supposed to broadcast the completion of their objective.

These factors aren't influenced by the visiting frequency of a prisoner, their visiting order, or the first switch's initial configuration. Upon the 44th switch-down by the leader, he will then know that everyone has already visited the room and has done their thing. In the case that it was originally in the down position, then the 22 prisoners would flip it up twice. In the case that it was originally in the up position, one prisoner would have to flip it up once, while the remaining 21 of them would have to do so twice.

Certainty can't be achieved amongst them regarding whether everyone has already done their part at least once after the leader flips the switch down 23 times, as the first 12 prisoners plus the leader could probably be brought to the room 24 times before anyone else does. In order to consider that the switch could have originally been switched up, it is necessary for the prisoners to flip up the switch twice. In the case that they flip it up only once, it would be unknown to their designated leader whether he is to count to 22 or 23.

(If we use an example of only 3 prisoners, it is necessary that the first switch would be flipped down thrice by their designated leader in order to ascertain that all the other prisoners have already gone into the room. This would equal out to be twice for the two other prisoners and once more in case the switch was originally in the up position.)

The Neighborhood

It is the German resident who owns the Green House, drinks coffee, and smokes Prince who has the fish as the pet. This is determined by process of elimination where the facts that are known are entered into a chart as shown below:

House	1	2	3	4	5
Color	Yellow	Blue	Red	Green	White
Natl.	Norwegian	Dane	Brit	German	Swede
Beverage	Water	Tea	Milk	Coffee	Beer

Smokes	Dunhill	Blends	Pall Malls	Prince	Blue Master
Pet	Cat	Horse	Birds	**Fish**	Dog

This chart is completed using the following criteria:

Nationalities:

1. Norwegian
2. Brit
3. Swede
4. Dane
5. German

House Colors:
1. Red
2. Green
3. White
4. Yellow
5. Blue

Beverages:
1. Tea

2. Coffee
3. Milk
4. Beer
5. Water

Cigars:
1. Pall Mall
2. Dunhill
3. Blends
4. Blue Master
5. Prince

Pets:
1. Dogs
2. Birds
3. Cats
4. Horses
5. Fish

How is the chart properly organized? It is determined simply by the logic of the statements provided. For instance, as the Brit is stated to live in the red house, no other nationality can live there; and as the Pall Mall smoker has a bird as a pet, no one else can smoke that cigar or have that pet. Once the already-determined statements have been filled into the chart accordingly, the only blank left over is where the pet Fish belongs, and the only remaining spot would be with the German residing the Green House who drinks coffee and smokes Prince.

The Game Show

You will have a better chance of winning the car if you decide to switch your choice of doors. This is because at your first choice, you had a 1 in 3 chance of choosing the right door. Therefore, you had a better chance of choosing the wrong door with your first guess. Now that you have had one door eliminated, you have a better chance of choosing the right door if you swap your choice since now, your odds of choosing correctly are 1 in 2.

This can be illustrated in the chart below:

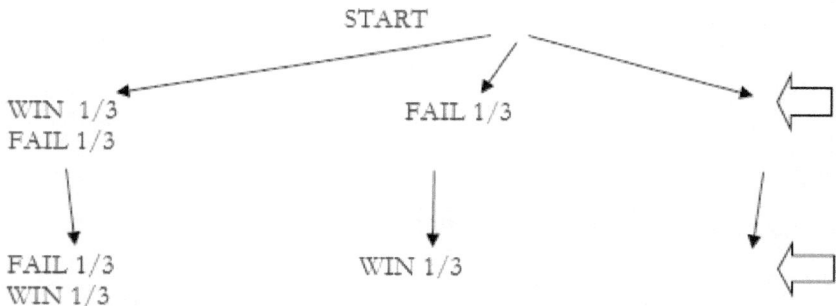

There are only three possibilities, each with a one-third probabilistic value. If you switch doors, your chance of winning is 1/3+1/3=2/3, and your chance of losing is 1/3.

Therefore, your chances of winning improve if you switch doors.

The Infinite Hotel

The announcement that the receptionist must make to all the current guests is to pack up and move down one suite to the left. This will ensure that the very first room in the hotel will now be vacant and can be rented to the lone guest.

Pirates

The captain is allowed to have 98 coins at most. How?

The captain announces that 98 coins will be taken by him, and one coin will be passed on to the third-eldest pirate and the last coin to the youngest pirate. Afterward, an explanation is provided in this way:

In the case that there were two pirates, with Pirate 2 being the oldest, he would just vote for himself, and that would result to fifty percent of the vote—hence, pretty much the entire money is safe with him.

In the case that there were three pirates, it is necessary for another pirate to be convinced by Pirate 3 to get involved in the plan. 99 gold coins would be taken by Pirate 3 and be given to Pirate 1. It is known to Pirate 1 that the only way that he gets something is through voting for Pirate 3, so he naturally sides with the said pirate's scheme.

In the case that there were four pirates, Pirate 2 would receive 1 gold coin from Pirate 4. For natural reasons, he votes for Pirate 4's scheme, as this is the only option that would give him something.

As there are 5 pirates on this pirate captain's crew, Pirates 1 and 3 will obviously have to vote for the captain—otherwise, they will get nothing and risk death.

Pirates II

In order for the captain to protect his own life, he suggests that the oldest pirate hand the coin to the youngest one. The captain uses logic similar to that of the first Pirates puzzle in explaining the vainness of any of the involved pirates attempting to take the coin.

The Greek Philosophers

The philosopher who stopped laughing was the second smartest philosopher out of the three. He stopped laughing because he realized that if his smartest colleague did not have anything on his head, then the third one was only laughing at him.

The Bar Fly

The man who entered the bar has a bad case of the hiccups. He first requests water to help relieve the hiccups, but drinking the water does not work. The bartender then pulls out a gun to startle the man and make his hiccups go away.

Conclusion

Thank you for making it through the end of *Karen's Logic Thinking Puzzles: Lateral Thinking Puzzles and Brain Teasers for All Ages*! Let us hope it was informative and able to provide you with all of the tools you need to achieve your goals in exercising lateral thinking—whatever they may be.

The next step is to simply keep trying out lateral thinking puzzles! You will find that there is often more than one way to come to the answer of many lateral thinking puzzles and that oftentimes, the puzzles that seem the most complicated are actually easily solved using simple logical thinking.

Lateral thinking principles have different applications in everyday life. One of the most common applications is in job interview questions, where the interviewer may ask a lateral thinking type of question to test how the candidate thinks under some judicious pressure.

Lateral thinking is a skill that can be learned. It is difficult to throw off the mentality that many of us have of "This Is the Way That I Have Always Done Things," and that is exactly what lateral thinking teaches. Imagine as if you are standing in front of a brick wall that is labeled *The Problem*. There is a set of footprints leading in a straight line right into the wall. You know that just beyond the wall is the *Solution*. You cannot follow the straight line of footprints any further because the straight line is leading you directly into the *Problem*. Hence, how do you solve it to get to the solution? Now, picture a path that leads you along the wall, then around a corner, goes into a few curves, and then ends up at the *Solution*. This is a literal interpretation of lateral thinking. It is using a different pathway than the straightforward logical path and is finding a new path towards the solution. Think about how you could utilize lateral thinking in dealing with other challenges in life.

An example of a lateral thinker in today's contemporary culture is the character MacGyver. MacGyver uses his lateral thinking skills to either find an escape, build a useful tool, or create a solution for negotiation time and time again—and in doing so, he always manages to outsmart the evil-doer. Any of MacGyver's methods show an extraordinary amount of understanding of lateral thinking and creating decisive action.

Finally, if you found this book useful in any way, a review on Amazon is always appreciated!

Thank you so much for reading, and I genuinely hope you enjoyed the journey!

Karen J. Bun

Connect with us on our Facebook page www.facebook.com/bluesourceandfriends and stay tuned to our latest book promotions and free giveaways.

Don't forget to claim your FREE book
https://tinyurl.com/karenbrainteasers

www.ingramcontent.com/pod-product-compliance
Lightning Source LLC
Chambersburg PA
CBHW020611220526
45463CB00006B/2543